Benefits of Brexit

A Comprehensive Analysis

Wilbert Wellington-Boot

DEDICATION

This book is dedicated to my great grandfather, Wilson Wellington-Boot. Wilson was an unsung British philanthropist who took great pride in his country. Amongst his many generous donations, he was a key financier of British colonialism in part made possible through his many successful business ventures

CONTENTS

'Brexit does mean Brexit.'
- Theresa May

CHAPTER 1

Standard of Living

CHAPTER 2

Health Care

Health Care

CHAPTER 3

Free Movement

Free Movement

.

CHAPTER 4

Economy

Economy

Economy

Economy

Economy

National Defence

CHAPTER 6

Foreign Trade

CHAPTER 7

Diversity

Diversity

Diversity

Diversity

Diversity

Diversity

Diversity

Diversity

Diversity

CHAPTER 8

Crime

Crime

Crime

Crime

Crime

Crime

Crime

CHAPTER 9

Employment

Employment

Employment

Employment

Employment

Employment

CHAPTER 10

Colour of Passports

Colour of Passports

THE END

ABOUT THE AUTHOR

Wilbert Wellington-Boot was born in to a decorated family whose lineage can be traced back to the inception of England. Through various trade and foreign financing ventures in the 1700s, the Wellington-Boot family amassed a small fortune which has to this day funded their philanthropy.

Wilbert briefly studied political sciences at University of Exeter online before pursuing a career in show horses. While in his prime, his equestrian career came to an abrupt end due to a tragic fox hunting accident. The fox escaped with only temporary emotional damage however Wilbert's injuries prevented him from ever mounting again. Despite being unable to ride, he still owns stables throughout Southern England as well as a significant stake in Elmer's Incorporated.

Whilst not busy promoting his writings or on tour for his lecture series *'Who is British and what does it mean?'*, Wilbert resides for much of his time on his Somerset estate where he enjoys sport hunting, masquerade parties and local courtesans.

THE
BENEFITS OF
SERIES

From politics and marriage, to childbirth and divorce, The *Benefits Of* series represents the life-time work of celebrated author Wilbert Wellington-Boot, whose unrivalled and encyclopaedic collection of studies has been published for generation after generation to enjoy.

For more comprehensive analysis of other topics, look no further than a *Benefits Of* book today.

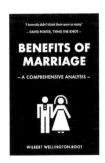

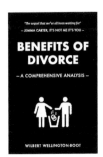

www.wilbertwellingtonboot.com